Unlocking the Secrets of Science

Profiling 20th Century Achievers in Science, Medicine, and Technology

Raymond Damadian and the Development of MRI

Marylou Morano Kjelle

Mitchell Lane
PUBLISHERS

PO Box 619 • Bear, Delaware 19701
www.mitchelllane.com

Unlocking the Secrets of Science

Profiling 20th Century Achievers in Science, Medicine, and Technology

Raymond Damadian and the Development of MRI

3/03

Mitchell Lane
PUBLISHERS

Copyright © 2003 by Mitchell Lane Publishers, Inc. All rights reserved. No part of this book may be reproduced without written permission from the publisher. Printed and bound in the United States of America.

Printing   1   2   3   4   5   6   7   8   9   10

Library of Congress Cataloging-in-Publication Data

Kjelle, Marylou Morano.

    Raymond Damadian and the development of MRI/Marylou Morano Kjelle.

      p. cm. — (Unlocking the secrets of science)

    Summary: Presents the biography of Raymond Damadian and the story of how he developed MRI (magnetic resonance imaging) technology and fought to protect his patent from infringement.

    Includes bibliographical references and index.

    ISBN 1-58415-141-2

    1. Damadian R. (Raymond), 1936- —Juvenile literature. 2. Magnetic resonance imaging—Juvenile literature. [1. Damadian, R. (Raymond), 1936- . 2. Scientists. 3. Inventors. 4. Magnetic resonance imaging.] I. Title. II. Series.

RC78.7.N83D3648 2002

571.4'092—dc21

    [B]   2002008323

ABOUT THE AUTHOR: Marylou Morano Kjelle is a freelance writer and photojournalist who lives and works in central New Jersey. She is a regular contributor to several local newspaper and online publications. Marylou writes a column for the *Westfield Leader/Times of Scotch Plains—Fanwood* called "Children's Book Nook," where she reviews children's books. She has written four nonfiction books for young readers and has an M.S. degree in Science from Rutgers University. For this book, Marylou personally visited with and interviewed Dr. Damadian.

EDITOR'S NOTE: Though the Unlocking the Secrets of Science series has been developed for young adults in the middle grades, this book requires an advanced interest and knowledge of science.

ACKNOWLEDGEMENTS: Special thanks to Raymond Damadian, M.D. and the FONAR Corporation, who cooperated with us in the development of this book.

PHOTO CREDITS: Unless otherwise noted, all photos are courtesy of Raymond Damadian, M.D. and the FONAR Corporation; p. 28 Corbis

PUBLISHER'S NOTE: In selecting those persons to be profiled in this series, we first attempted to identify the most notable accomplishments of the 20th century in science, medicine, and technology. When we were done, we noted a serious deficiency in the inclusion of women. For the greater part of the 20th century science, medicine, and technology were male-dominated fields. In many cases, the contributions of women went unrecognized. Women have tried for years to be included in these areas, and in many cases, women worked side by side with men who took credit for their ideas and discoveries. Even as we move forward into the 21st century, we find women still sadly underrepresented. It is not an oversight, therefore, that we profiled mostly male achievers. Information simply does not exist to include a fair selection of women.

Contents

Dr. Raymond V. Damadian, inventor of magnetic resonance scanning, poses in front of his history-making prototype named Indomitable *used to make the first MR image of a human on July 3, 1977. The machine is now on permanent display at the Smithsonian Institutions's Hall of Medical Sciences.*

Chapter 1

A Diagnostic Revolution

● ●

A persistent headache, a lingering cough, a pain in the stomach that won't go away. As recently as 25 years ago, doctors had no definitive means of diagnosing the medical conditions that cause such symptoms. Today, a diagnostic test called magnetic resonance imaging (MRI) allows doctors to diagnose diseases by viewing scans of the body's internal organs. Patients can now be diagnosed, treated and cured of illnesses that at one time might have incapacitated or killed them. The person who discovered the principals of MRI and built the first MRI scanner is Dr. Raymond V. Damadian.

When Raymond Damadian was a student at the Albert Einstein College of Medicine in New York, he planned to specialize in internal medicine. He enjoyed solving puzzles and knew a career as an internist would provide many opportunities to play detective as he identified diseases.

However, by the time Raymond Damadian was in medical school, he had decided to work in medical research instead of in a medical practice. He knew he could help more people with one significant laboratory discovery than he could ever treat as a physician.

Raymond Damadian did not set out to develop magnetic resonance imaging. As a young professor at Downstate Medical Center in Brooklyn, New York, he used nuclear magnetic resonance (NMR) to measure potassium concentration in halophiles, salt-loving bacteria from the Dead Sea. He was studying the way electrolytes—sodium and potassium—cross over the bacteria's cell membrane. For these ion-exchange experiments, he used an instrument called the nuclear magnetic resonance spectrometer.

Nuclear magnetic resonance is a physical phenomenon in which magnetic fields and radio waves cause atoms to give off tiny signals. Before Raymond Damadian's research began in the late 1960s, many physicists and chemists had used NMR to investigate the chemical properties of various types of matter. However, none of the scientists had made the connection between NMR technology and its ability to externally detect disease within the human body.

Damadian knew there were differences in ion exchange between normal and cancer cells. He hypothesized that an NMR scanner could be developed to externally detect cancer within the live human body, the same way it could detect chemical changes in halophiles.

From the early 1900s on, cancer was detected primarily by two methods. Both had drawbacks. The X ray, invented by Wilhelm Conrad Roentgen in 1895, showed bones clearly, but often missed diseases of the body organs because of its inability to generate image contrasts of soft tissue. In the early 1970s two inventors working independently, Godfrey Newbold Hounsfield and Allan MacLeod Cormack, invented an X-ray machine that used a computer to demonstrate clear cross-sectional views of the human body. The computerized axial tomography (CAT) scan exposed the patient to increased doses of radiation, yet was also unable to detect cancer in soft tissues.

Raymond Damadian saw a way he could link NMR technology and medicine. With fierce determination, he set out to bring the two branches of science together.

When Raymond was 10 years old he watched his maternal grandmother die slowly and painfully of breast cancer. "I think that's when he got it into his head that he wanted to cure cancer," Raymond's mother said of that time.

Using the principles of NMR, Raymond Damadian built a scanner large enough to study the entire human body. Doctors now have a way to image internal organs without exposing their patients to exploratory surgery, harmful dye injections or excessive radiation. The scanner, called a nuclear magnetic resonance scanner, produced a nuclear magnetic resonance image.

As is often the case with those who chart a new course, Raymond Damadian faced obstacles. He had difficulty getting funding for his research. When he couldn't afford to buy the components to make the first human-body scanner, he built what he needed or used things others had discarded.

Some of the researchers of the time laughed at Damadian's idea of a human-body scanner. They said it couldn't be done. There were mechanical problems as well. The canister holding the liquid helium needed to cool the magnet was plagued with vacuum leaks. Then, when he attempted to scan his own body by nuclear magnetic resonance, he received no signal. Damadian was too large and had overloaded the antenna that was used to pick up NMR signals.

After spending several frustrating weeks studying different coil designs, one of Damadian's graduate students, Larry Minkoff, volunteered to enter the scanner. He was the first person to undergo successful magnetic resonance scanning. The date was July 3, 1977.

In 1978, Damadian founded the FONAR Corporation to manufacture and sell MRI scanners to hospitals and clinics. His success brought its own worries. Large manufacturers of diagnostic equipment saw the value of the MRI scanner and set out to copy his technology and manufacture and distribute their own. Damadian fought, and won, patent infringement battles within the legal system. As a result, he would become an advocate for the independent inventor and America's entrepreneurial spirit.

Thousands of MRI scanners are presently in use in hospitals and clinics worldwide. Improved technology has made magnetic resonance scans so precise that the interior of the human body can be viewed in intricate detail, allowing the smallest cancers to be detected.

MRI scanning has been called a diagnostic revolution. In addition to cancer, MRI scans now detect diseases of the brain, spinal cord, heart and kidney. Millions are alive today because of Raymond Damadian and his MRI scanner.

Dr. Raymond Damadian is often referred to as the "Father of Diagnostic NMR" for his development of the Magnetic Resonance Scanning, which led to his invention of Magnetic Resonance Imaging (MRI) using whole body scanners. Dr. Damadian's invention has been credited with saving millions of lives.

Chapter 2

"Always Doing Something"

• •

Raymond Damadian was born in Manhattan on March 16, 1936. He was the first child of Vahan and Odette Damadian. Raymond's Armenian father had narrowly survived the Turkish persecutions in the early 1900s. In 1920, at 17 years old, he immigrated to America; he married Odette Yazedjian in 1932. Odette was part French and part Armenian. Her father had come to the United States in 1906, settled in New York, and set up the country's first Renault car distributorship.

Vahan worked as a photoengraver for the *New York World* (later to become the *New York World-Telegram*). Shortly after Raymond's birth, the family moved to Queens, another borough of New York City. They eventually settled on Austin Street in the Forest Hills section of Queens. Before Raymond was two years old, his sister, Claudette, was born.

Raymond spent his childhood in a working-class neighborhood, far from the well-to-do families that also lived in Forest Hills. His neighbors, like his parents, stressed the importance of obtaining a good education and adhering to a strong work ethic. This was a common upbringing among children whose parents and grandparents had immigrated to America.

When Raymond was five years old, America went to war. The United States entered World War II after Japan bombed Pearl Harbor on December 7, 1941.

Raymond attended Public School 101, where he was an excellent student. His mother remembered him as "always interested in something creative—drawing, reading, building. Everything was creative. He was always doing something. He could never sit still. If he did, he was reading."

When he was five years old, Raymond began studying the violin. Although he hardly practiced, he played well. When he was eight years old, the Juilliard School of Music in Manhattan accepted him. He studied there for eight years. His violin instructor described him as a kind and honest young man who exhibited a lot of confidence in himself.

Raymond also sang in the children's choir and played violin at the services of his Congregational church.

At the age of 12 Raymond began taking tennis lessons at the Forest Hills West Side Tennis Club. He excelled at the sport and played junior tennis on the West Side team, including the Jr. Davis Cup competitions. He took tennis competition seriously, an early indication of the determination and resolve he would need many years later as a research scientist.

In many ways Raymond was an average teenager. He held summer jobs to earn extra spending money. He worked at a rug-cleaning factory, but lugging heavy wet rugs was tough, very dull and very dusty. Occasionally he could be found behind a pile of carpets, napping to regain his energy. Another summer Raymond worked behind the counter at a local Howard Johnson Restaurant. He also sold cutlery and Fuller brushes door to door.

He was a well-behaved young man who always got along with his sister, Claudette. The only problem he gave his parents was coming home after his curfew. His father avoided punishing Raymond; it was his mother who was the disciplinarian. She said: "My discipline was to put them in their room . . . to Raymond discipline didn't matter much, because he would just take out a book or do some work. He was never at a loss for something to do. I never knew whether sending him to his room did any good."

Raymond's father worked from midnight to 8:00 A.M. at the *World-Telegram* and was able to spend a lot of time with his son. It was from his father that Raymond received his self-confidence. Vahan impressed upon Raymond that he could do anything he set his mind to.

The work of many scientists before Raymond Damadian had significant influence in the field of medical diagnoses. But the major discovery of the 20th century came in 1895 when Wilhelm Conrad Roentgen, shown here, discovered x rays. These new rays made it possible to see "beneath the skin," and to diagnose many medical problems without invasive surgery.

In the 1970s, two inventors working independently, Alan M. Cormack (bottom, left) and Godfrey N. Hounsfield (bottom, right) each developed the concept that x rays could be managed by computer to better give cross-sectional views of the human body. Their research was responsible for computerized axial tomography or CAT scans.

Dr. Damadian adjusts the readings of his oscilloscopes while conducting early experiments in Magnetic Resonance Scanning research.

Chapter 3

A Grandmother's Inspiration

● ●

Raymond excelled in math and science at Forest Hills High School. When he was 15, he applied for a Ford Foundation Scholarship. It was based on academic excellence, and recipients of these scholarships were allowed to enter college before finishing high school. The scholarship offered full tuition and room and board at one of four universities: the University of Wisconsin, the University of Chicago, Columbia and Yale.

Ten thousand students countrywide took the Ford Foundation's national board examinations. The first round of tests narrowed the field to 1,000 finalists. A second round of testing selected the 200 winners. Fifty went to each of the four universities. The University of Wisconsin selected Raymond.

Raymond had to choose between the three loves of his life: the violin, tennis and science. Accepting the scholarship meant walking away from a career as either a musician or a professional tennis player. He was particularly concerned about the violin. Should he accept the scholarship and forget about a career in music? Should he turn down the scholarship, finish high school and continue on at Juilliard?

"We didn't have the financing for college. If I didn't accept the scholarship, it would not have been possible to go away at all to a university," said Raymond. He decided in favor of the University of Wisconsin. He was 16 years old when he arrived at the Madison campus in the fall of 1952. Raymond majored in mathematics and minored in chemistry.

By the time he was in his third year of college, he knew he wanted to go to medical school. His grandmother Jeanne's death from cancer in 1946 was an influencing factor. He had been especially close to her. She doted on her grandson, and, despite speaking very little English (French was her native language), she was a loving yet strict influence in Raymond's life.

Her death from cancer impressed upon Raymond that training in medicine would give him the ability to relieve suffering. "For a long time I couldn't understand that she was going to die. I wanted her to get well. Her suffering had a strong impact on me. I had an early exposure to the ravages of cancer and saw it inflict agony in a way that very few do. I saw very clearly what that horrid disease could do to someone you loved," said Raymond.

"When I became a medical doctor, cancer was the disease I always seemed to be focused on," he said.

After receiving a bachelor's degree in mathematics in 1956, Raymond returned to New York and entered Albert Einstein College of Medicine.

Medical school did not come as easily to Raymond as high school and college had. Years later it was his creative brain he held responsible for his difficulties. "Medical schools are highly disciplined environments that put a creative person to work as a student. I had a lot of trouble reconciling the information presented to me in medical school and the math and physics I had learned as an undergraduate," he explained.

Raymond would have preferred to spend his summers doing research at Einstein, but financial pressures forced him to take summer jobs. In 1956, the summer before he started medical school, he became a tennis teacher at the Dune Deck Hotel in Westhampton, on eastern Long Island. He made $2,500 for the summer, which was quite a sum of money in 1956.

While working as a tennis instructor, Raymond met his future wife, Donna Terry. Donna worked behind the soda fountain counter at Speed's Pharmacy in Westhampton, a place Raymond would drop by while on break from teaching tennis. She was studying pre-nursing at Houghton College in upstate New York. She eventually received her RN degree from Columbia University. A week after Raymond graduated from Albert Einstein College of Medicine, he and Donna were married. The Damadians eventually had three children: Timothy, Jevan and Keira.

By the time he was finishing his residency and fellowship in internal medicine, Raymond had selected a career path of medical research over private practice as a physician. A genuine concern for others and a willingness to work hard to make a contribution to the science of medicine was behind his decision.

"I realized that a scientist who goes into the laboratory has the capability to help millions of people," he said. "I didn't know if anything would come of any research I might do, but I knew I wanted to try to alleviate the medical suffering of millions of people instead of the relatively few I could bring relief to with treatments at the bedside."

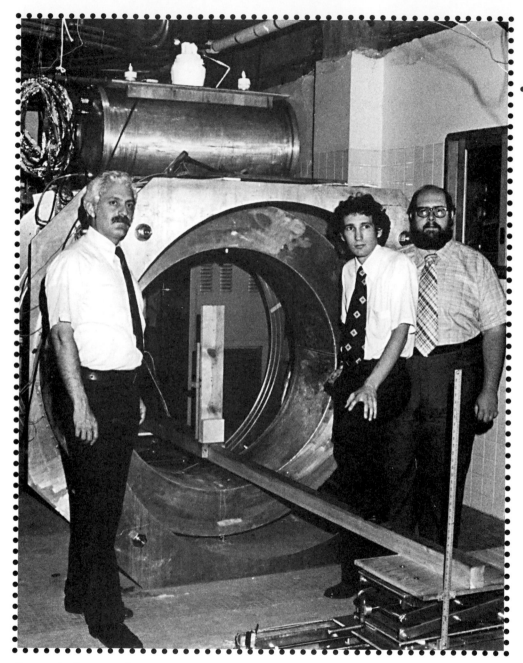

From left to right: Dr. Raymond Damadian, Dr. Larry Minkoff, and Dr. Michael Goldsmith pose beside Indomitable. *Dr. Damadian met Minkoff and Goldsmith when he was on the faculty of Downstate and Minkoff and Goldsmith were graduate students there.*

Chapter 4

Searching for the Sodium Pump

• •

Damadian completed his internship and residency in internal medicine at the State University of New York's Downstate Medical Center in Brooklyn, New York. (Downstate has since been renamed State University of New York Health Science Center at Brooklyn). His main area of interest was the balance of fluids and electrolytes in the human body.

From Downstate, Damadian went to Washington University School of Medicine in St. Louis as a postdoctoral fellow in nephrology, the study of the kidneys, in the renal division of the Department of Internal Medicine. He studied with Dr. Neil Bricker, a well-known scientist who was researching the effects of disease on the kidney.

At Washington University, Damadian began wondering whether he should undertake a search for the sodium pump, the mechanism believed to be responsible for sodium reabsorption in the kidney. Although it had never actually been found, the sodium pump had been discussed in the work of scientists who had received the Nobel Prize.

Proving that the sodium pump existed was exactly the type of challenge Damadian craved. In 1963 he transferred to Harvard Medical School, where Professor Arthur Solomon was conducting research on the alkali ions, sodium and potassium, and studying their metabolism.

While at Harvard, Damadian had the opportunity to audit a quantum physics course taught by one of the pioneers of NMR research, Nobel Prize winner Edward Purcell. Years later, the significance of NMR principles would enter into Damadian's work.

Damadian developed a strain of mutant *E. coli* bacteria that lacked the mechanism for potassium transport across the cell membrane. Studying the bacteria, he tried to isolate the protein molecule responsible for sodium and potassium transport.

Damadian's research was interrupted when he was called into the Air Force. He reported to Brooks Air Force Base and the School of Aerospace Medicine in San Antonio, Texas. While serving his country as a captain in the medical corps, he was allowed to continue his search for the sodium pump. At the same time, he had to conduct experiments on the toxicity of the liquid rocket propellant hydrazine for the United States government.

While at the School of Aerospace Medicine, Damadian began to doubt the existence of the sodium pump. In experiment after experiment, he failed to find convincing evidence for its existence.

"I looked to find evidence in my own experiments that would support the existence of the postulated sodium pump. Gradually I began to question the existence of a sodium pump," Damadian recalled. Now his research took a 180-degree turn. Instead of trying to discover the sodium pump, Damadian conducted experiments to try to determine if it even existed.

In 1967 he returned to Downstate and became a member of the faculty of the Department of Internal Medicine and the Program in Biophysics. As part of his responsibilities to the medical school, Damadian taught biophysics to graduate students. In return, he was given a laboratory on the sixth floor of the university hospital.

With the help of two graduate students, Michael Goldsmith and Larry Minkoff, Damadian studied the composition of sodium and potassium in cells. In a study of the cell's energy mechanisms, the team disproved the sodium pump theory. The cell did not have enough energy to run a sodium pump.

Damadian had his own theory of cellular ion transport. He believed the material inside the cell was arranged into a semiorganized molecular structure. He also believed it was the electrical charges of atoms on large immovable molecules inside the cell, and not a pump, which held ions such as potassium within the cell. "If an atom fits into this macromolecule structure, the cell holds it. If it doesn't fit, then it passes out of the cell," Damadian hypothesized.

An important component of Damadian's theory rested on the substance water. Because a charged particle attracts water, it will always have a water covering. Larger ions attract less water than smaller ions because they have less charge per unit of surface area. The cell keeps the molecule that is the smallest size when fully encased in its water atmosphere. The potassium ion is a smaller molecule than sodium when fully encased; therefore, if a cell has to choose between hydrated potassium and hydrated sodium, it will keep the potassium and expel the sodium. Damadian called his theory of cellular ion exchange the ion exchange resin theory.

In February of 1976, Dr. Damadian produced the first scan of a live animal—a mouse with cancer—by focusing the NMR signal and scanning the interior of the animal.

Chapter 5

The Detection of Cancer

• •

At a meeting of the Federation of American Societies of Experimental Biology held in 1969 in Atlantic City, New Jersey, Damadian was introduced to Freeman Cope. Cope was studying the electrical conductivity of biological systems at the United States Naval Air Development Center in Warminster, Pennsylvania. He was using an instrument called a nuclear magnetic resonance (NMR) spectrometer to obtain his results. The instrument belonged to the manufacturer, the Nuclear Magnetic Resonance Specialties Corporation, located outside Pittsburgh in New Kensington, Pennsylvania. The president of the company, Cope informed Damadian, generously let scientists use his equipment.

After measuring sodium in the brain and kidney, Cope was about to attempt potassium measurements by NMR. He knew potassium's signal was weaker and would therefore be more difficult to detect. Damadian offered to help by acquiring halophile bacteria from the Dead Sea of Israel. These bacteria were known to have an extraordinarily high potassium content.

In the summer of 1969, Damadian and Cope loaded their cars with electronics and bacteria-growing equipment and headed up the Pennsylvania Turnpike to Nuclear Magnetic Resonance Specialties Corporation. Damadian was about to be introduced to nuclear magnetic resonance.

Damadian handed Cope the Dead Sea bacteria he'd grown in giant fermentation flasks the night before at the University of Pittsburgh. Cope inserted them into the NMR spectrometer. The signal on the oscilloscope was instantaneous. The variable that translates into an oscilloscope reading is the time it takes the atoms to return to equilibrium after they have been stimulated by a pulse of radio energy. This period of time is called relaxation or decay

Dr. Damadian (left) with Dr. Freeman Cope. Cope first introduced Damadian to the workings of an NMR machine in 1969 while they were performing spectroscopy experiments on potassium-rich bacteria at NMR Specialties in New Kensington, Pennsylvania.

time. Damadian and Cope were the first to measure the potassium content of biological tissue by NMR.

Damadian was eager to use the NMR technology to test his ion exchange resin theory on cancer cells. When cancer cells start growing out of control, they take over the internal mechanisms of normal cells. A cancer cell fills up with water, loses its ability to exclude sodium and frequently has a low potassium concentration. Damadian postulated that the different water structure between normal and cancer cells should translate into a difference in relaxation times.

Anticipating the application of NMR technology to human cancer detection, Damadian began cancer studies with rats. In June 1970 he returned to NMR Specialties alone. Using tissue from rats with Walker sarcoma, he compared the relaxation times of hydrogen protons of cancerous tissue with normal tissues.

In a presentation to the Washington Patent Lawyers Club in 1992, Damadian described the experiments: "After a few more days of measuring normals . . . I decided to attempt the cancer measurement. To my mind, this was the measurement that would make or break my NMR body scanner idea. I needed that abnormal cancer signal if there was to be any hope of a human scanner that could hunt down cancer deposits within the body. I held my breath and made the first measurement. It was different—dramatically different."

Damadian understood the implications of his discovery. If rat cancer tissue could be detected in a test tube by an NMR spectrometer, then with a large enough magnet, NMR applied to the whole body in a scanning format should detect a difference in relaxation times between cancer tissue and normal tissue within the body. NMR could be used as a means of detecting cancer in the live human body.

After repeating the studies, Damadian published his results in a paper entitled "Tumor Detection by Nuclear Magnetic Resonance" in the journal *Science* on March 19, 1971. The paper was the first to put forth the idea that disease in humans could be externally detected by means of NMR. Damadian used his results that diseased and normal tissues exhibited different relaxation times to come to this conclusion. Damadian's *Science* paper was the most widely cited publication in the field of MRI from 1970 to 1989.

Damadian had proven it was possible to distinguish cancer tissue from normal tissue using NMR. Once he realized NMR's potential, he envisioned it expanding beyond cancer, helping to diagnose heart disease, strokes, kidney disease and a whole host of other illness.

Dr. Damadian is shown here in the early days of the FONAR Corporation conducting MRI experiments during the development of the medical industry's first commercial scanner, FONAR's QED 80.

Chapter 6

Chemistry by Wireless Electronics

● ●

T he first time Damadian saw an NMR spectrometer in action at Nuclear Magnetic Specialties Corporation in 1969, he thought of it as "doing chemistry by wireless electronics."

The science behind the technology of Damadian's "wireless atomic electronics," as he also called it, had actually begun in the late 1930s when Dr. Isador I. Rabi, working with a graduate student, Norman F. Ramsey, at Columbia University passed a beam of lithium chloride molecules through a magnetic field. When the beam was later bombarded with radio waves, molecular beam magnetic resonance resulted. Rabi was awarded the 1944 Nobel Prize in physics for his discovery.

In 1945, two research groups, working independently of one another, were the first to demonstrate nuclear magnetic resonance in condensed matter. The scientists heading these groups were Edward M. Purcell of Harvard University and Felix Bloch of Stanford University. They shared the 1952 Nobel Prize in physics.

Rabi's experiments dealt with isolated molecules. Studying the proton—the nucleus of the hydrogen atom—Purcell and Bloch observed magnetic resonance in liquids and solids. Their research provided the basic principle upon which nuclear magnetic resonance theory in naturally occurring samples rests.

Atoms consist of protons and neutrons, which are inside the nucleus, and electrons, which are outside the nucleus. The nuclei of most atoms have an odd number of protons and neutrons. Most have a property called spin. The spin of protons and neutrons add together, giving the nuclei a net spin, like a miniature toy top.

In 1945 Dr. Felix Bloch, working at Stanford University, was one of two researchers who discovered the phenomenon of Nuclear Magnetic Resonance. The principles of NMR soon became the analytical foundation upon which studies of the composition of chemical compounds were based. In 1952, Dr. Bloch was awarded the Nobel Prize in Physics for his work.

When the atom is in a normal state, the little spinning tops are randomly oriented. When the atom is exposed to an external magnetic field, the field exerts a force on the magnetic poles of the spinning nuclei and tries to line up the miniature tops in the magnetic field as they spin.

Instead of actually lining up bolt upright, however, they wobble, or gyrate. This wobbling is called precession. It is the same precessing motion exhibited by a spinning top as it avoids falling by circling around a center point with its axis at an angle. As the precessing spinning atoms line up, they divide into two separate groups. One group is made up of those atoms whose precessing spins align with the direction of the magnetic field. The second group consists of those atoms whose precessing spins oppose the magnet's field. Those atoms whose spins align with the direction of the magnetic field have a lower energy level than the group whose atoms oppose the magnetic field.

When a radio wave, similar to the one that might initiate at a radio station, is beamed at right angles to the magnetic field, the wobbling nuclei in the group whose spins align with the magnetic field absorb the energy of the radio wave. Absorption causes them to flip their orientation and jump up in energy. The atoms boosted to the higher energy level by the stimulating radio waves get in line, or resonate, with those of the second group, whose atoms normally oppose the magnetic field. This transition is described as the nuclear magnetic resonance phenomenon.

Depending upon the magnetic strength of the nucleus and the strength of the magnetic field, each type of atom (e.g., hydrogen, sodium, nitrogen, etc.) wobbles at its own frequency. This frequency is called the atom's resonant frequency, or Larmor frequency.

Once all the atoms have reached the higher energy level, the stimulating radio wave is shut off. The excited atoms will then slowly realign themselves with the magnetic field and return to the lower energy group. As they return, the energy that was absorbed by the nuclei when they were excited is emitted.

The resonant frequency of a given nucleus can shift when its atomic neighborhood changes. The amount of energy emitted is directly proportional to the concentration of emitting nuclei in a given area. Using a radio receiver and an antenna, the resonance signal can be transferred to an oscilloscope. The strength of the nuclear signal can therefore be directly measured.

Bloch studied the amount of time it took for the nuclear signal to decay and return to equilibrium after the nuclei were excited by the radiofrequency. He called this decay time the nucleus' relaxation time. Two time quantities governed this decay time. They are T_1 and T_2. T_1 indicates spin-lattice relaxation. It is the interaction between the nucleus and its environment (lattice).

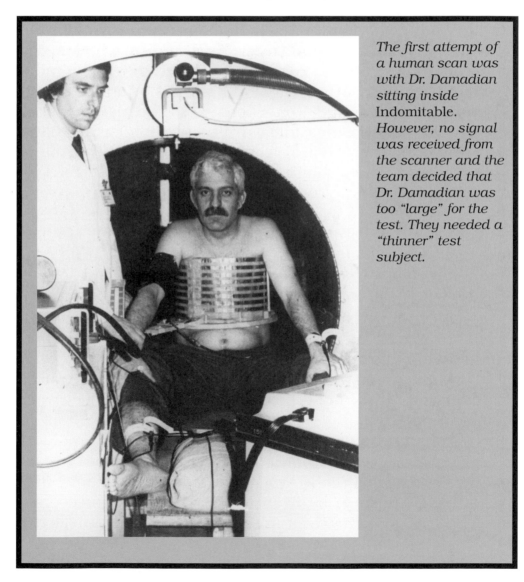

The first attempt of a human scan was with Dr. Damadian sitting inside Indomitable. *However, no signal was received from the scanner and the team decided that Dr. Damadian was too "large" for the test. They needed a "thinner" test subject.*

T_2 is called spin-spin relaxation. It describes the interaction between a given nucleus and its neighbors of the same nucleus type. The physical environment of the nucleus influences T_1 and T_2. In 1948, Purcell and Pound, along with Nicholas Bloembergen, published a paper on nuclear magnetic relaxation.

The entire basis of the diagnostic properties of nuclear magnetic resonance is based upon this discovery—that normal tissue and diseased tissue display different T_1 and T_2 values. There would be no useful NMR images either on an oscilloscope or computer monitor without the marked differences in the decay (relaxation) of the nuclear resonance signal in diseased and normal tissues. If the relaxation differences did not exist, all the image pixels of the MR image would have the same (or about the same) pixel intensities. The image would be a blank.

In the late 1940s, Henry Torrey at Rutgers University in New Jersey and Edwin Hahn at the University of Illinois, working independently, substituted pulses of radio waves instead of a continuous long wave. In 1949, Hahn discovered the "spin echo" phenomenon. Spin echoes were attributed to the speeding up and slowing down of the spinning nuclei due to variations in the local magnetic fields.

Rabi, Ramsey, Purcell, Bloch, Bloembergen, Torrey and Hahn gave the world the scientific discoveries that led to the discovery of NMR. But it was Damadian, looking at the phenomenon through the eyes of a physician and not a physicist, who saw the implications NMR could have for the detection of disease in humans.

In 1988, Dr. Damadian received the National Medal of Technology, the nation's highest honor in technology, from then-President Ronald Reagan. In giving the award, President Reagan cited Dr. Damadian "for his independent contributions in conceiving and developing the application of magnetic resonance technology to medical uses, including whole-body scanning and diagnostic imaging."

Chapter 7

The World's First NMR Scanner

Damadian's first NMR study of potassium and his later studies of rat tumors were done on samples contained in test tubes. To scan a human, Damadian proposed moving a magnet across the body of the patient. The magnet would provide the necessary focus. In addition, the radio field could be shaped to provide additional focusing. If abnormal tissue were present, its signal would be different from the surrounding normal tissue.

Damadian planned to take advantage of the saddle point feature present in the magnetic field of most magnets to accomplish the needed focusing of the NMR signal. When the radio frequency was applied, only the atoms present in the saddle point region, where the magnetic field was fairly constant, would produce significant signal. The tissue signal outside the region would decay too quickly to contribute to the overall signal from the region. The nuclear resonance signal would be focused.

The magnet's saddle point was called the sweet spot. The sweet spot would be tuned so that its strength produced a resonance whose frequency matched the center frequency of the stimulating radio frequency pulse. The radio frequency would also be shaped (focused) so that it would have the strength needed to fully excite only the tissue atoms located at the sweet spot. In this way the focusing available from the magnet's saddle point and the focusing available from the radio transmitter and receiver would combine to create a single focused spot of a desired size.

The result would be a focused resonance that would be capable of distinguishing signals from different parts of the body. Damadian called this technique FONAR, or *field focused nuclear magnetic resonance*.

On March 17, 1972, Damadian applied for a patent describing the first device ever for scanning the human body by magnetic resonance. It was one day after his 36th birthday. In the patent application, Damadian described using the T_1 and T_2 relaxation times of atomic nuclei in biological tissue to detect in vivo cancer in the human body.

Damadian was searching for funding for his NMR work. After being turned down by the National Institutes of Health (NIH), he wrote to President Richard Nixon. Nixon had declared a war on cancer and had allocated one billion dollars a year for three years for cancer research. In his letter to the President, Damadian called the rejection of his proposal a "colossal stupidity."

Damadian could never be sure his letter to the President had an influence, but he was invited to reapply for NIH money and received a grant of $20,000 each year for three years. With the money he purchased an NMR spectrometer and a superconducting magnet.

On February 5, 1974, Damadian was granted patent number 3,789,832 for "Apparatus and Method for Detecting Cancer in Tissues." The same year, NIH awarded him $100,000 a year for three years to study the reliability of an NMR signal in differentiating normal, benign and malignant tissues with the ultimate objective of performing scans of living samples.

To obtain tissue samples for his work, Damadian would send a graduate student by taxi to Memorial Sloan-Kettering Cancer Center in Manhattan. Before his study was completed, Damadian's lab had studied over 1,000 human tissue samples.

In February 1976, Damadian produced the first scan of a live animal—a mouse with cancer—by focusing the NMR signal and scanning the interior of the animal.

When word got out that Damadian was planning to scan humans, his colleagues joked and poked fun at his research. NMR scientists spun their test tube samples in a

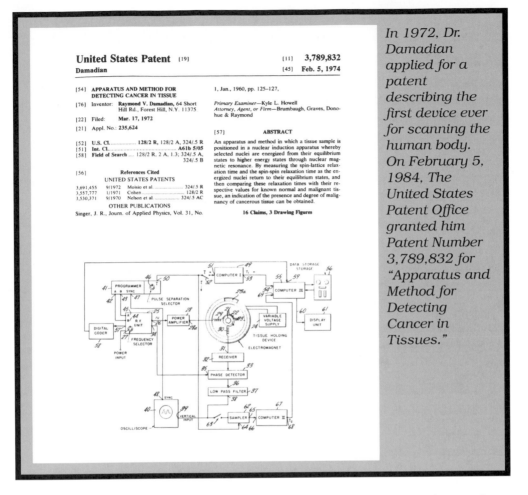

ABSTRACT

An apparatus and method in which a tissue sample is positioned in a nuclear induction apparatus whereby selected nuclei are energized from their equilibrium states to higher energy states through nuclear magnetic resonance. By measuring the spin-lattice relaxation time and the spin-spin relaxation time as the energized nuclei return to their equilibrium states, and then comparing these relaxation times with their respective values for known normal and malignant tissue, an indication of the presence and degree of malignancy of cancerous tissue can be obtained.

16 Claims, 3 Drawing Figures

In 1972, Dr. Damadian applied for a patent describing the first device ever for scanning the human body. On February 5, 1984, The United States Patent Office granted him Patent Number 3,789,832 for "Apparatus and Method for Detecting Cancer in Tissues."

centrifuge prior to obtaining their readings. Damadian often heard the question, "How fast do you propose to spin the patient, doctor?"

Using a computer program named Mag Map from Brookhaven National Laboratories, Damadian designed the human magnet. He and his team began construction of a human-sized superconducting magnet capable of generating a 5,000-gauss magnetic field. Damadian's magnet design called for a Helmholtz pair of magnets to make the magnetic field as uniform as possible. Goldsmith was in charge of building the magnet. It was to be composed of two hoops, each 2.5 inches thick and 53 inches in diameter. Goldsmith used rolled channel bar for their construction. Channel bar is U-shaped and made of aluminum. When it is rolled into a circle, it provides a form for layering wire in a coil—the basis for making a magnet.

Each of the two hoops consisted of 30 miles of precisely wound niobium-titanium superconducting wire. Wires of two different diameters were needed. The wire would be laid in 52 layers. There were 76 to 91 turns in each layer.

An old metal bookcase found in a heap of discarded furniture became the rack for the winding machine. Motors found in a bargain store on Canal Street on the southern tip of Manhattan were hooked up to spin the hoops as they were wound with the wire. The wire was fed through a small thimble.

Achieving the calculated magnetic field called for by the design specifications required a perfect magnet and nonresistant wiring. There was no way of testing the wire as Goldsmith wound it. He ran an ohmmeter up and down and across the hoops to find shorts in the magnet. When he was at last satisfied, he wrapped insulation around the hoops.

Goldsmith completed his part of the project months before Damadian and Minkoff, who were building the dewars. The dewars were each 10 feet tall, 6 feet wide and eighteen inches deep. Each would weigh one and a half tons.

Each dewar was really a set of three doughnuts fitting one inside the other. The smallest one would contain the magnet and be filled with liquid helium. The doughnut in the middle was made out of aluminum and would be filled with liquid nitrogen, which would keep the helium cooled. Wrapped with 851 layers of super-insulation, the doughnut would also repel radiation. The largest doughnut was a one-half-inch-thick aluminum vacuum can. This had to be free of air, which could transfer heat and warm the helium. A special vacuum removed all air molecules. A tank to hold extra helium was one of the last parts of the dewar to be constructed.

In a constant race against time, Damadian abandoned his plan to use the Helmholtz pair of magnets of his original design and decided to proceed with one magnet. Fearful that another scientist would produce a human magnetic resonance image before they did, the group worked seven days a week, often until two or three in the morning. Many nights Damadian didn't leave the lab at all.

Damadian calculated he needed $200,000 to complete the project. Running short of money, he made an unsuccessful trip to Plains, Georgia, to ask president-elect Jimmy Carter to help secure the funds to continue the project.

In the end, it was four private investors—Bill Akers, Clark Akers, John Rich and Jim Stewart of Nashville, Tennessee—each contributing $10,000, that gave Damadian the financial backing needed to complete the prototype NMR whole-body scanner.

Damadian's original design for a human-body scanner called for the patient to remain stationary and the magnet to move across the body. It soon became clear that it would be easier if the magnet remained stationary and was made large enough for the patient to be moved across the sweet spot. A movable wooden platform was built for the patient to sit on while being scanned.

The scanner design called for the patient to wear a probe or coil to allow for the transmission of the stimulating radio waves. The coil would also act as an antenna. It would be attached to a coaxial cable that would be attached to a radio transmitter while the body's atoms were being stimulated by radio waves. It would be switched to a receiving antenna at the moment the body was emitting radio signals that could be received. A radio-receiving coil had to have a tuning capacitor to generate a signal.

By trial and error, Goldsmith built antennas from coils and capacitors. To induce the antenna to resonate at the right frequency of the sample, it had to be matched with the right set of capacitors. On his 50th try, Goldsmith produced an antenna that produced a signal. It was 14 inches in diameter and constructed of copper foil tape and cardboard he'd found in the garbage.

As a committed Christian, Damadian relied heavily on his faith to get him through the scanner's development. Throughout the months of racing to be the first to perform a human scan, Damadian also found solace in his wife's support. In their book about the history of MRI, Mattson and Simon recorded, "All she could do was pray. It was rare when her Bible was not close at hand and its tattered pages were with the notes needed to provide her husband scriptural wisdom and support when she perceived the need. Except that she was an extraordinary woman of faith, we could not have stayed the course. She had to endure the anxieties and then raise the children alone."

Even though the NMR had been used on animals with no ill effects, there was reason to be concerned about scanning a human. In terms of stored energy, Damadian's magnet was the ninth largest in the world—the eight larger magnets were all part of nuclear accelerators. A 5,000-gauss magnet would surround the subject while radio beams were aimed at the subject's body. (Before the first actual human scan, the magnetic field was reduced to 500 gauss. One reason was that the lower field was deemed safer for the first human try.)

Damadian volunteered to be the first human to be scanned. He approached the first human-body MRI scanner with an electrocardiogram attached to his chest to monitor his heartbeat, a blood pressure cuff on his right arm, and an electroencephalogram wired to his head. Nearby stood a cardiologist, an EKG, a canister of oxygen, and a cardiac defibrillator. Damadian, Goldsmith and Minkoff were well prepared in the event the magnetic field adversely affected Damadian's body.

In this first attempt to scan a human with MRI, no resonance signal was received from Damadian.

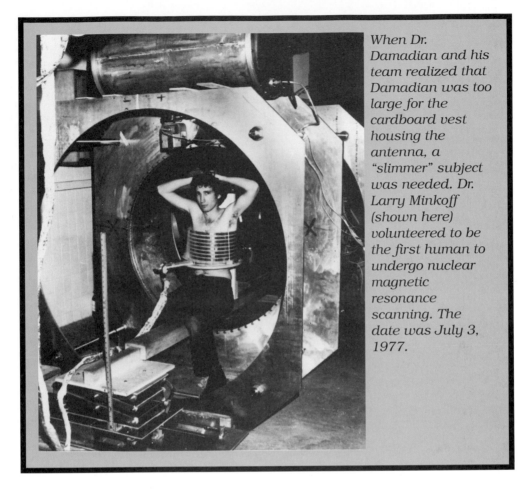

When Dr. Damadian and his team realized that Damadian was too large for the cardboard vest housing the antenna, a "slimmer" subject was needed. Dr. Larry Minkoff (shown here) volunteered to be the first human to undergo nuclear magnetic resonance scanning. The date was July 3, 1977.

The scientists came to the conclusion that Damadian was too large for Goldsmith's coil, so they were unable to obtain a radio signal. On July 2, 1977, Minkoff, a slimmer fellow, volunteered to be scanned. There was an immediate signal from Minkoff's chest. A computerized interpolation produced the first image of the live human body by the morning of July 3, 1977. It was known as MINK-5.

Damadian wrote in Goldsmith's notebook, "Fantastic Success! 4:45 A.M. First Human Image Complete in Amazing Detail showing heart, lungs, vertebra, musculature."

In honor of the spirit in which it was created, Damadian named the scanner Indomitable.

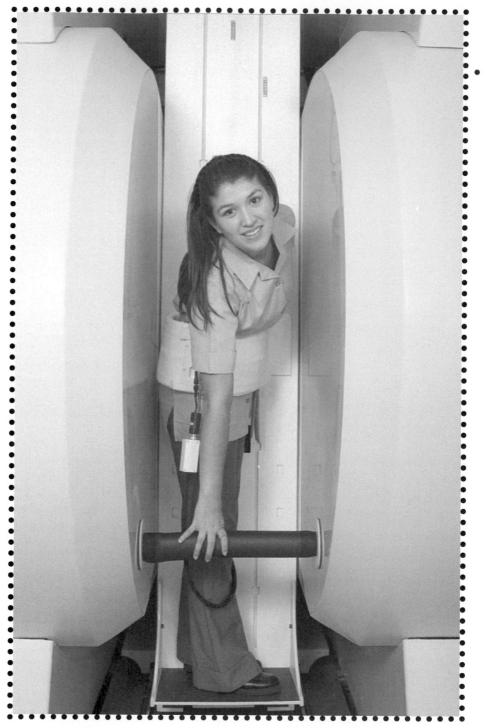

In 2001 FONAR introduced the Stand-Up™ MRI, the world's first whole-body MRI able to scan a patient in standing, sitting, or lying down position.

Chapter 8

The Father of Diagnostic NMR

●●

The story of the development of NMR for use as a diagnostic tool is a story of two separate sciences—physics and medicine—and how they were brought together by one man for the good of all people. Because Dr. Raymond V. Damadian took his understanding of physics and applied it to medicine, countless numbers of people the world over owe their lives to him and his MRI scanner.

From the very beginning, it had been Damadian's intention for magnetic resonance scanners to contribute to the detection of disease. In 1978, nine months after Minkoff's whole-body MR image was produced by Indomitable, Damadian incorporated FONAR Corporation. He and his brother-in-law, David Terry, set out to raise $2.5 million, the amount of money Damadian projected it would take to launch the business. Thirty-five individuals, including Damadian, invested in the company. Damadian invested his life savings, the sum he had been able to put aside from his professor's salary. He wanted all the investors to know that if they lost their money, he would lose his as well.

Before FONAR was incorporated, Damadian made a design change to the scanner. The superconductive magnet that needed constant cooling by expensive liquid helium and liquid nitrogen wasn't practical for hospital use. Damadian changed the magnet in the scanner from superconductive to permanent.

Other changes were made to make the product more attractive and versatile for the consumer. A bed was designed. An outside shell was constructed of fiberglass.

The first MRI human scanner, the QED 80, was ready for sale in March 1980. A patient entered the scanner lying on a patient bed. A radio pulse was transmitted into the region of anatomy being scanned. When the radio energy was turned off, the antenna picked up the radio signals given off by the atoms of the body's tissues. The radio signals were then sent to a computer, which projected them as a picture on a computer screen. The QED 80's price tag was $550,000.

Aware that many hospitals and clinics could not afford an MRI scanner, Damadian worked to make them more affordable to hospitals, and more available to patients. In 1983, FONAR introduced a mobile scanner, allowing hospitals and clinics that could not afford to purchase a scanner to share one.

FONAR's first scanners provided only a bird's-eye view of what was to be the ultimate impact of NMR in the diagnostic field. As time went on, Damadian's MRI scanners would become progressively better and faster. As image quality improved, new diseases and regions of the body were added to its list of detection capabilities.

Once MRI's value in diagnosing disease was established, large corporations entered the market by manufacturing and distributing their own MRI scanners. In 1984, Damadian sued Technicare Corp., a division of Johnson and Johnson, for patent infringement. This was the beginning of many years of legal battles for Damadian and FONAR.

In 1995 a jury awarded $110 million to FONAR for patent infringement by General Electric. A judge overruled part of the decision, but in 1997 a United States Court of Appeals affirmed the entire judgment in favor of Damadian, proving FONAR to be the first in the field of MRI. FONAR received payment for the judgment from General Electric on July 3, 1997, twenty years to the day that marked the world's first MRI scan. FONAR subsequently settled patent infringement lawsuits with Hitachi, Philips, Siemens, Toshiba and other corporations.

In addition to holding the pioneer patent for MRI scanning, and producing the first whole-body MRI scan, Damadian counts among his achievements the first open

MRI scanner, and the permanent magnet technology to achieve it. In all, Damadian holds over 40 patents.

On July 15, 1988, at a ceremony at the Executive Offices of the White House, President Ronald Reagan awarded Damadian the nation's highest honor in technology, the National Medal of Technology. It was awarded to Damadian for his "independent contributions in conceiving and developing the application of magnetic resonance technology to medical uses, including whole-body scanning and diagnostic imaging."

In 1989 Damadian was inducted into the National Inventors Hall of Fame, joining Thomas Edison, Alexander Graham Bell, the Wright Brothers, Samuel Morse and the other giants of invention history. The Hall of Fame is located in the U.S. Patent and Trademark Office building in Washington, D.C., and in Inventor Place, Akron, Ohio. At the time of Damadian's induction, President George Herbert Walker Bush cited Damadian as "living, reassuring proof that the spirit of invention continues to thrive in our great Nation."

Damadian has also been the recipient of the National Engineers' Special Recognition Award, the Lawrence Sperry Award and the American Creativity Lifetime Achievement Award.

In 2001, FONAR introduced the Stand-Up™ MRI, the world's first whole-body MRI to scan the patient in the weight-bearing position. The Stand-Up™ MRI can scan the patient standing, sitting, lying down or in other positions.

Today there are over 10,000 MRI scanners in use worldwide. Indomitable, the very first NMR machine to scan the live human body, is on permanent exhibit in the Hall of Medical Sciences at the Smithsonian Institution in Washington, D.C.

Raymond Damadian Chronology

1936 Raymond Damadian born on March 16

1946 grandmother dies of breast cancer

1951 applies and receives Ford Foundation Scholarship

1952 enrolls at University of Wisconsin at the age of 16

1956 receives bachelor's degree in mathematics from University of Wisconsin; enrolls at Albert Einstein College of Medicine in New York

1960 receives M.D. from Albert Einstein College of Medicine; begins internship and residency in internal medicine at the State University of New York's Downstate Medical Center in Brooklyn; studies the role of the kidney in regulating electrolyte balance in the body; marries Donna Terry

1962 becomes a postdoctoral fellow studying kidney sodium reabsorption at Washington University School of Medicine in St. Louis, Missouri

1963 begins research on the sodium pump at Harvard Medical School

1965 enters Air Force; continues to conduct research on the sodium pump and to perform experiments on hydrazine

1967 returns to Downstate Medical Center as a member of the faculty of the Department of Internal Medicine; develops ion exchange resin theory to explain transfer of electrolytes across membranes

1969 meets Freeman Cope at Federation of American Societies of Experimental Biology in New Jersey; using an NMR spectrometer, Cope and Damadian are the first to measure potassium content in biological tissue by NMR; makes first proposal ever of NMR body scanner in a grant application to Health Research Council of the City of New York

1971 publishes "Tumor Detection by Nuclear Magnetic Resonance" in *Science*

1972 applies for first patent ever for scanning the human body by NMR

1974 receives patent for NMR scanner; NIH awards him $100,000 a year for three years to develop the scanner

1976 produces an NMR scan of a live mouse

1977 Larry Minkoff, a graduate student working with Damadian, becomes the first human to undergo magnetic resonance screening

1978 incorporates FONAR to develop and manufacture NMR scanners

1980 the first commercial NMR scanner, the FONAR QED 80, becomes available for patients

1982 FONAR introduces and installs open MRI technology

1984 NMR scanners receive clearance from the FDA

1988 receives the National Medal of Technology from President Reagan

1989 inducted into National Inventors Hall of Fame

1992–1998 fights and wins patent infringement battles

2001 FONAR introduces and installs the Stand-Up MRI

Magnetic Resonance Imaging Timeline

1895   Wilhelm Roentgen discovers X rays

1930s   I. I. Rabi and Norman F. Ramsey discover molecular beam magnetic resonance by shooting a beam of lithium chloride molecules through a magnetic field, then subjecting it to radio waves

1945   Working independently, Edward Purcell and Felix Bloch demonstrate nuclear magnetic resonance in condensed matter

1948   Nicholas Bloembergen, Edward Purcell and Robert Pound publish their studies on nuclear magnetic relaxation

1949   Henry Torrey and Edward Hahn, working independently, discover "spin echo" phenomenon

1971   Godfrey Hounsfield and Allan MacLeod Cormack build the first computerized tomography (CT or CAT) scanner; Raymond Damadian discovers the NMR relaxation differences in cancer tissues and proposes the NMR body scanner; he publishes "Tumor Detection by Nuclear Magnetic Resonance" in *Science*

1972   Paul Lauterbur obtains the first magnetic resonance image of solutions in capillary tubes; Damadian applies for first patent for scanning the human body by NMR

1974   Damadian receives patent number 3,789,832 for NMR scanner

1977   Damadian and colleagues perform the first NMR scan of Larry Minkoff

2002   Over 10,000 MRI scanners are in hospitals and clinics worldwide

For Further Reading

Books

Damadian, Raymond V. "The Story of MRI," address delivered to the Washington Patent Lawyers Club in Washington, D.C., February 10, 1992.

Kleinfield, Sonny. *A Machine Called Indomitable.* New York: Times Books, 1985.

Mattson, James, and Merrill Simon. *Pioneers of NMR and Magnetic Resonance in Medicine: The Story of MRI.* Jericho, N.Y.: Dean Book Co., 1996.

Zannos, Susan. *Godfrey Hounsfield and the Invention of CAT Scans.* Bear, Del.: Mitchell Lane Publishers, 2002.

Magazines

Brice, James. "MRI Pioneer Assesses His Scientific Legacy," *Diagnostic Imaging*, September 1996.

Damadian, R. V., et al. "Tumor Detection by Nuclear Magnetic Resonance," *Science*, March 19, 1971.

Schneider, David. "Profile: Raymond V. Damadian," *Scientific American*, June 1997.

Web Sites

Magnetic Resonance Imaging by Joseph P. Hornak, Ph.D.

http://www.cis.rit.edu/class/schp730/lect/lect-2.htm

The Invention Dimension Inventor of the Week: Raymond Damadian

http://web.mit.edu/invent/www/inventorsA-H/damadian.html

Chickscope: MRI Introduction for High School Students

http://chickscope.beckman.uiuc.edu/about/overview/mrihs.html

FONAR

http://www.fonar.com

Glossary of Terms

Atom: the smallest particle of an element that can undergo change in a reaction. Atoms consist of protons and neutrons, which are inside the nucleus, and electrons, which are outside.

Capacitor: an element in an electrical circuit used to temporarily store charge.

Condensed matter: matter in liquid or solid state.

Decay time: the amount of time it takes for a signal from a nucleus to return to equilibrium (also known as relaxation time).

Dewar: a container that stores liquefied gases such as helium at low temperature so that they can be used in scientific experiments.

Diagnostic test: a test used to identify a disease.

EKG (electrocardiogram): a recording of the electrical activity of the heart.

Electrolyte: a chemical compound that ionizes and becomes electrically conductive; sodium and potassium are examples of electrolytes.

Equilibrium: a state of balance in which reactions are equal.

Helmholtz pair: a pair of electric coils set apart by one coil diameter to maximize the uniformity of the magnetic field between them.

In vivo: in a living body.

Ion: an atom, part of an atom, or group of atoms with a charge: electrons are ions with a negative charge, and protons have a positive charge; neutrons have no charge, so are not ions.

Ion exchange: a mechanism of exchange of ions across a cell membrane within a living cell or within an ion exchange resin bead.

Larmor frequency: the precession frequency of a spinning atomic nucleus as it precesses, or wobbles, around the direction of the applied magnetic field.

Magnetic field: a field of force that exists around a magnetic body.

Magnetic resonance: the absorption of radiofrequency energy by atomic particles such as the atomic nucleus when placed in a magnetic field and then stimulated by a radio transmission.

Magnetic resonance imaging (MRI): the use of magnetic fields to create internal anatomical images from the resonance of atomic nuclei.

Mutant: a new trait or organism that arises from genetic change.

Nuclear magnetic resonance (NMR): a phenomenon of physics in which magnetic field and radio waves cause atoms to give off tiny radio signals.

Ohmmeter: an instrument that measures electrical resistance.

Open MRI: an MRI scanner in which the patient's view is not obstructed.

Oscilloscope: an instrument that provides images of electrical quantities.

Permanent magnet: a magnet that retains its magnetism after being removed from an electric current or magnetic field.

Pixel: the picture element from which computer images are constructed.

Precession: the wobbling of spinning nuclei around the axis of the magnetic field when the atom is exposed to a magnetic field.

Proton: the nucleus of a hydrogen atom.

Radio wave: an electromagnetic wave in the radiofrequency range.

Saddle point: a region within a laboratory magnet where the field has maximum uniformity (that is, minimum variation).

Sodium pump: the mechanism by which it was believed ions traveled across cell membranes; Damadian questioned the existence of the sodium pump.

Spectrometer: an instrument for measuring the frequency of nuclear magnetic resonance.

Spin: the rotation of the nuclei within atoms. The net nuclear spin is the sum of the spin of the atom's protons and neutrons.

Spin echo: a resonance signal that arises when the spinning nuclei in a sample come into phase with each other.

Spin-lattice relaxation (T_1): the time to reach energy equilibrium between the nucleus and its environment.

Spin-spin relaxation (T_2): the time for nuclei of the same type to get out of phase with each other.

Superconductive magnet: an electromagnet in which the flow of current encounters zero electrical resistance.

Sweet spot: the magnet's saddle point wherein the magnetic field uniformity is greatest.

Tomography: the production of three-dimensional images of structures inside the body.

Index